A panda cit

Created by Sumeet Mohan

This book belongs to:
_____

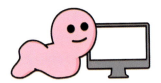

© 2024 Sumeet Mohan
www.apandacitis.com

The right of Sumeet Mohan to be identified as the author of this work has been asserted by him in accordance with the Copyright, Design and Patents Act 1988. Without limiting the rights under copyright reserved above, no part of this publication may be reproduced, stored in or introduced into a retrieval system, or transmitted, in any form or by any means (electronic, mechanical, photocopying, recording or otherwise), without prior written persmissions of the copyright owner.

Information for parents:
The experience of going to hospital varies for every child. This book is designed to be both entertaining and educational, by exploring the hospital experience through an adventure story. Please consult a medical professional, should you or your child have any medical queries or concerns.

ISBN: 9798398377347

To everyone who looked after me when I had appendicitis and to those who encouraged me to create this book about my experience.

Atop the Sunken Summit, Pembroke the panda was ready to start a day filled with adventure.

But as he ran outside, Pembroke felt a pain in his tummy that made him shout…

"Mummy! Daddy! My tummy really REALLY hurts", cried Pembroke.

"Don't worry," said Daddy Panda, "we'll take you to see the Doctor".

So, off they went to the hospital...

Inside the hospital, the Panda family had to wait for a l o n g,   l o n g time.

Pembroke did not mind waiting, because he found a rollercoaster toy to play with.

Finally, a Doctor and Nurse came out to see the family.

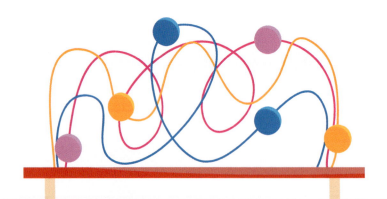

"We heard that your tummy's been hurting, so we are going to do some tests to find out why" said Doctor Hoot.

"But I don't like tests" moaned Pembroke, "we have to do those at school!"

"No Pembroke, this is a different type of test" explained Nurse Otto.

The Doctor poked and prodded Pembroke's tummy, which made him say "OUCH!" all over again.

Then, the nurse used a very skinny needle, to take some blood from Pembroke's arm.

"The tests are done" explained Nurse Otto, "now we just have to wait for the results."

white blood cell

Red blood cell

In another room, a very clever scientist used a microscope to look at Pembroke's blood.

By zOOMING in, the scientist could see Pembroke's blood cells very clearly.

This helped the doctor to work out why Pembroke's tummy might be hurting.

"Your tests show that you have Appendicitis," explained the Doctor.

"What's a-panda-citis?" asked Pembroke.

"It's when a part of your tummy called the Appendix becomes poorly. We have to take it out, to make you feel better. And don't worry Pembroke, you don't need your Appendix!"

The Doctor told Pembroke that he was not allowed to eat anything before the operation.

Then, Pembroke changed into a hospital gown, which reminded him of a superhero cape.

After some time, his bed was pushed down the corridor.

In the next room, the Doctor placed a special mask over Pembroke's mouth and nose.

The Doctor then asked Pembroke to count as high as he could.

"1. 2.. 3...", counted Pembroke, "4.... 5..... 6.............."

And with that, Pembroke was fast asleep!

In his sleep, Pembroke dreamt that he was crossing a bridge towards a ginormous castle.

But, Pembroke could hear a strange sound coming from the top of the castle. So, he ran inside and up the stairs.

As he reached the top, Pembroke was shocked to see who was shouting...

… it was his appendix!

"Oh Pembroke, I'm in ever so much pain! I've been tangled up for so long!" cried the Appendix, "won't you set me free?"

Suddenly, Dr Hoot swooped down from the sky and cut the Appendix down.

"I am so sorry for all of the trouble I have caused you. Now that I am free, I will not bother you anymore," promised the Appendix, before it left the castle and walked off into the distance.

As he watched the Appendix leave, Pembroke began to wake up from his dream...

Pembroke woke up in the hospital with Mummy and Daddy Panda by his side.

They told him that his tummy would start to feel better soon and that he could go home in a few days.

It turned out that Pembroke got to have an exciting adventure after all!

Printed in Great Britain
by Amazon